Test your

Aptitude and Ability

Test your

Aptitude and Ability

GARETH LEWIS

Series editors: GARETH LEWIS & GENE CROZIER

Hodder & Stoughton

A MEMBER OF THE HODDER HEADLINE GROUP

Orders: please contact Bookpoint Ltd, 39 Milton Park, Abingdon, Oxon OX14
4TD.
Telephone: (44) 01235 400414, Fax: (44) 01235 400454. Lines are open from 9.00
– 6.00, Monday to Saturday, with a 24 hour message answering service.
Email address: orders@bookpoint.co.uk

British Library Cataloguing in Publication Data
A catalogue record for this title is available from The British Library

ISBN 0 340 78005 3

First published 2000
Impression number   10 9 8 7 6 5 4 3 2 1
Year   2004 2003 2002 2001 2000

Copyright © 2000 Gareth Lewis

Typeset by Fakenham Photosetting Limited, Fakenham, Norfolk.
Printed in Great Britain for Hodder & Stoughton Education, a division of
Hodder Headline Plc, 338 Euston Road, London NW1 3BH by Cox & Wyman
Ltd, Reading, Berkshire.

Contents

Introduction

Within the *Test Yourself* series we cover a wide range of skills, competencies, capabilities and styles. Some of these can be measured by objective tests that we call psychometric tests. Others can be assessed or evaluated using a variety of other methods.

Those that are usually tested directly with psychometric tests fall into two major groups. The first group focuses on aspects of typical performance. These measure aspects of our preferences, style and developed habits. Tests of personality fall into this category. The second group focuses on aspects of maximum performance. These are the tests of aptitude and ability that we cover in this book.

This group of tests are very important for a number of reasons:

- They represent a wide range of skills and abilities that can be tested.
- Most assessment processes involve one test of aptitude or ability.
- People fear these tests more than any others.

This last point is quite important – because these tests seek to measure aspects of our abilities and talents that other people judge us by and by which we judge ourselves.

This book is designed to explain and reassure. We will set out what exactly it is that these tests measure, and how this is done. We will describe some of the most often used tests.

We will give you a chance to 'have a go' and to get a good idea of your own performance. Finally, we will explain how these tests fit in with the repertoire of other kinds of test, and what use is made of the information.

In this book we look at:

- Why aptitude and ability are important
- Aspects of aptitude and ability
- Testing aptitude and ability
- Test your own ability
- Interpreting your scores
- Developing your aptitude and ability

Why aptitude and ability are important

In this first chapter we shall look at some important questions about the subject of aptitude and ability. We will do this by asking some basic questions:

- Why do organisations use testing?
- Why are aptitude and ability important?

Why do organisations use testing?

Psychometric testing is increasingly being applied in many of the Human Resource functions. These include:

- selection and recruitment
- training needs analysis
- training and development
- team development
- change and culture initiatives
- performance management
- career counselling.

Probably the most important situation in which organisations test people is when they are recruiting staff. The reasons for this are not hard to fathom. It has been estimated that it can cost upwards of £100,000 to recruit and train an executive or graduate member of staff. Poor recruitment and selection can have many adverse consequences. In other words, the costs of making a mistake can be very high. It is worth saying that putting the wrong person in the wrong job also has poor consequences for the individual involved as well as for the organisation. Small wonder then that organisations seek more efficient and cost-effective methods to help them.

If you think about this situation from the point of view of the organisation, obviously their main priority is to find out as much as they can about the individual and match that information to the known requirements of the job. From the individual's point of view, they need to know and understand the process involved, and also know what it is the organisation is looking for. Finally, they also need to know how they measure up to the requirements. This book should provide information and answers to all of these.

An organisation can only match information about candidates to their own requirements if they have worked out in some detail what the requirements of the job are. In most organisations there are two ways to describe these requirements:

1 *The job description*. This describes the roles and responsibilities of the job and the individual tasks that should be undertaken. It focuses on the job itself.
2 *The person specification*. This describes the range of knowledge, experience, skills and qualities that the holder of the job needs to have in order to fulfill the job description successfully. As the name implies, it focuses on the individual.

In the standard recruitment process (although we shall see later that there are many variations on this), the organisation will have information from three sources:

1 curriculum vitae (CV) – a document describing the candidate's employment experiences and qualifications

2   interviews – the candidate's behaviour and answers to
    questions
3   references – testimonials about a candidate from third
    parties.

Each of these in turn suffers from some important weaknesses
from the point of view of the organisation. The reasons are
not hard to see. For instance, take interviews. Interviews are
notoriously unreliable as a means of selecting people. There
are many reasons for this. They may be constructed wrongly
– the wrong questions get asked, or different individuals get
asked different questions so making comparisons between
candidates is difficult. Interviewers may not be trained and
therefore may not have the appropriate skills. Interviews are
known to be highly subjective – interviewers make up their
mind about candidates very quickly and based on dubious
information. The criteria against which candidates are judged
can be wrong, and may not relate too closely to the
requirements of the job.

Organisations are also becoming aware that using flawed or
inaccurate information can lead to mistakes. And mistakes,
as we have pointed out, are expensive. The disadvantages
of poor selection:

1   higher turnover of staff
2   poor performance and stress
3   poor morale
4   high costs related extra costs of recruitment.

Not surprisingly then, organisations look for more objective
and accurate information to support their selection
decisions.

Other applications

As mentioned above, aptitude and ability tests are not only used for the purposes of recruitment and selection. They can also help to enhance a whole range of other Human Resource functions.

Here are just a few.

Progression
For many of us in working environments, moving on to the next job involves a leap in the dark. Historically, people have tended to be promoted to new positions with more responsibilities and seniority because we are good at what we are currently doing. That is, we are promoted because of the skills and abilities we showed in our old role. However, these are very often not the skills and abilities that are required in the new role.

Management is a very good example of this. Many people get promoted to a management position because they are good at something else. How many good teachers have gone on to become poor headteachers? Such situations are a double whammy because, at once, we lose the skills of the teacher as well as having to contend with the headteacher who may not have the appropriate skills.

In these situations, testing does not (or should not) replace the need for other data to be taken into consideration. Information about experience, performance and qualifications still have a role to play. Testing can contribute an extra dimension of information that may not be obvious from these other sources. They can provide detailed and standardised data in relation to specific skills (such as the ability to manipulate complex data, or to handle numerical data) or to deeper, underlying aptitudes.

Organisations are becoming more intelligent in identifying the abilities that help to promote people to where they can function with success.

Advisory/counselling
In many ways, this is a similar story to that above. Testing can help to build a rich picture of strengths and weaknesses in the context of career counselling. Whether this is done internally within an organisation, or by some outside agency, it tends to happen at a watershed in a person's career. By having a wider range of information, the choices can be evaluated more objectively.

Assessment for development
There has been a substantial growth in recent years in the use of assessment in relation to development and learning activities. This has also resulted in a subtle shift from testing by organisations for the benefit of organisations to assessment done in partnership with the individuals involved and at least as much for the benefit of the individual themselves.

Aptitude and ability tests can play a part in such processes, although they are also likely to involve tests of typical performance such as personality tests, team role profiles and many others.

Why are aptitude and ability important?

Information about aptitude and ability is one of the ways that organisations can satisfy the requirement of being more objective and more accurate, as set out above. Later on we find out how the information is made more accurate and more objective. There we discuss the testing process, and answer questions about how the information is acquired.

For the moment, we need to look in a little more depth at why aptitude and ability are important. We can do this by looking at a few typical job roles:

Job 1 Receptionist

Key Tasks

- Greet visitors and look after them in reception area until escorted into the workplace.
- Contact members of staff when they have visitors.
- Manage the visitors' pass system.
- Operate the switchboard in a helpful, friendly and courteous manner.
- Receive deliveries and organise mail.

Job 2 Service Engineer

Key Tasks

- Organise a repair visits rota.
- Repair equipment efficiently and effectively.
- Sell replacement equipment where appropriate.
- Order spare parts.
- Manage the team.

Job 3 Community Regeneration Director (Local Government)

Key Tasks

- Seek sources of inward investment.
- Liaise with other directors and chief executive.
- Identify job creation opportunities.
- Manage regeneration programmes.

Each of these jobs in turn require different skills, knowledge and experience. Some of these skills are very directly dictated by the job itself and the work involved. So, for each of them, for instance:

Receptionist

- Experience of using the phone and switchboard.
- Knowledge of the pass system.
- Knowledge of incoming delivery procedure.

Service Engineer

- Ability to construct rotas.
- Selling skills.
- Technical knowledge of equipment and tools.
- Knowledge of ordering process.
- Management skills.

Regeneration Director

- Understanding of political framework.
- Experience of regeneration initiatives.

- Knowledge of central government and EU funding sources for programmes.

None of these descriptions are complete, but you can probably add some elements of your own to each job description. Similarly, for some of these it is reasonably easy to check if people have the knowledge, experience and skills by examining their track record and experience and their qualifications.

However, for each of these there are some underlying skills and abilities that candidates will clearly need to be successful at these jobs. Let's look at the Regeneration Director.

Some of these skills will be described in the person specification. Here is what they look like:

- leadership
- communication skills
- working effectively in teams
- judgement and analytic skills
- political skills
- determination
- supportive management style.

This person is going to need to be of above average intelligence with the ability to understand highly complex issues and to think laterally to achieve objectives.

Can you derive a similar list for each of the other two job descriptions?

Even in lists like this we can see that there are a few

separable categories. For instance, those that are more to do with social behaviour in normal day-to-day situations we talk of as being 'typical' performance. They describe our approach and personal style of behaviour in a range of circumstances. They are more to do with our personality. Our personal preferences influence how we relate to other people in our management and leadership style. They influence our determination, assertiveness and so on. These will be dealt with in the book *Test Your Personality* in this series.

For some of the items on this list we need to know more about a person's learnt skills or their innate or underlying skills and potential. These are the areas that we are concerned with in aptitude and ability.

We can see why they are important – because they underwrite many aspects of our performance or potential performance at work. They are also the skills that are most difficult to identify from the more traditional recruitment processes described above.

Summary

We have argued in this chapter that organisations have a need to make the recruitment process more efficient, more cost effective and fairer. In order to do this they need more objective data, and this is where psychometric testing in general becomes useful.

Via a few examples we have established that there are underlying abilities that contribute to the successful performance of any type of job role. What we now need to do is to be a little more specific in describing the nature of these underlying abilities.

Aspects of aptitude and ability

In this chapter we shall describe in detail the range of aptitude and abilities that can be evaluated and tested. To do this we shall look at:

- The difference between general intelligence, aptitude and attainment
- The key aspects of ability

If you think about the whole range of ways in which people interact with the world around them it doesn't take long to realise that we develop an incredible range of skills over a lifetime. We use a massive repertoire of abilities just to get on with our daily lives.

Some of these skills are perceptual – like vision. Others are physical and involve strength, stamina and bodily control. For most work-related applications, however, it is the cognitive or mental skills that are by far the most important.

Because there is such a wide range of abilities within this general term that can be tested they are grouped and classified into various categories. We will describe some of the major categories here. First, let us look at the kinds of abilities that can be categorised and therefore tested.

Ability tests

This is the generic name for all tests of maximum performance. But within the whole category there are different types of test:

- tests of general or fluid intelligence
- tests of overall or underlying aptitude
- attainment tests.

Intelligence (IQ)

For most of this century it has been assumed that there is some single over-arching innate capability that underwrites our ability to learn and master most cognitive skills. It was called IQ for intelligence quotient. Psychometric testing really began with the notion of intelligence testing.

On the whole, the original notion of IQ has now been discredited. Psychometricians (psychologists interested in measuring ability) use the notion of 'fluid intelligence' to explain that our ability to learn or master one specific area is related to our ability to master any other.

There are tests that focus on and attempt to measure this fluid intelligence. The line of reasoning is clear. If we know your score on such a test, we can infer your ability to perform a whole range of cognitive tasks. That is then a good basis for predicting other abilities. We will come to look at these tests later.

Aptitude

There is another school of thought that says that we should look at more specific aspects of general cognitive ability. As well as giving more detailed information, these specific abilities are more closely work related, and from them we can predict more accurately a person's likely performance in work tasks.

These measure natural ability or potential to learn a skill or a set of skills. They focus on our underlying ability, but applied in specific areas. They should not require specialist knowledge or learning.

So what does get measured? Here are some typical things that get measured:

- **Abstract reasoning** – assesses the ability to understand the relationships between shapes and figures.
- **Verbal reasoning** – assesses understanding of words and relationships between words.
- **Numerical reasoning** – assesses the ability to operate on numbers and numerical concepts.
- **Critical reasoning** – assesses the ability to draw inferences from data of various kinds.
- **Accuracy tests** – assess the ability to check or classify information. Checking computer statements or syntax would be an example.

Other more specific types of test include:

- mechanical reasoning
- spatial reasoning
- hand–eye coordination.

Attainment

The aptitude tests are distinct from attainment tests. These measure skills and/or knowledge which have already been learned or acquired. They test the ability to put that knowledge to use. This is intelligence applied and learnt in a specific context. They can test quite specific tasks and abilities and can be highly work related. Examples might include:

- typing tests
- new written test for learner drivers
- spelling tests
- grammar and punctuation tests

We should also mention that some of the tests that are apparently tests of aptitude, can also involve a substantial learnt element. This means that strictly speaking, they are also tests of attainment. Tests of mechanical ability fall into this category where aptitude and attainment overlap.

The key aspects of ability

As we set out above, ability can be broken down into various categories. However, from our individual point of view, the three categories of:

- verbal
- numerical
- abstract

are by far the most important. They are the ones that are focused on, in terms of testing, in most organisations. They also, together, comprise a rounded and comprehensive selection of a person's general ability as it relates to work-based skills.

This is not to say that in some specific jobs other abilities may not be required. Throughout this book there are examples where other abilities, such as mechanical or spatial ability, might be important. However, this trio seems to be the ones that are required, to a greater or lesser degree, in most jobs. Therefore, in our discussions, and in our testing section, we shall concentrate on them.

In the sections that follow, we shall describe the abilities in terms of what is usually tested for in the common and widely available tests.

Verbal ability

What is verbal ability?
It is your understanding of words and the relationships between words. At the highest level, tests of verbal ability test the ability to reason with words.

What are verbal ability tests used for?
Using words is at the basis of so many of our work-related skills. Whether it be spoken or written, most of us have to have and to develop a facility with words, in order to make sense of the world and to communicate well. These skills are particularly relevant in jobs that involve a great deal of communication. These include sales, any aspect of customer service, including telesales. For similar reasons, nearly all senior executive posts and all management positions will involve both verbal and written communication as a core set of skills.

How is it tested?
These types of test come at a number of levels. They can be:

Spelling, grammar, vocabulary. As such they are nearer to attainment tests, rather than tests of aptitude. They can also include tests of accuracy. These are justified where the skills tested are a necessary component of the job in question. Data entry would be an example. Secretarial jobs requiring people to write letters or other forms of written communication are also relevant. Finally, some jobs in Information Technology require attention to detail and accuracy in data manipulation.

Comprehension/relationships between words. These are the most common type of tests to look at verbal aptitude, and can be used for a whole range of jobs that involve verbal (or written) communication.

Verbal critical reasoning. This is the 'highest' level which looks at reasoning and logical argument. These types of test are relevant where people have to deal with large amounts of complex data and argument and particularly where they have to draw inferences or conclusions from them.

Types of question (item)

A major factor in overcoming anxiety for many people is knowing what to expect. To help with this, we shall look at the typical types of question (or item, as it is called) that appear in tests.

In tests of attainment the questions take a fairly predictable form, depending on the type of attainment in question. Among the most common are questions on **spelling**:

? Test Yourself

1 Choose the correct spelling:
accommodate accommadate acomadate acommadate

Completing sentences correctly:

2 Choose the correct word to complete this sentence:
They did not bring .... money with them.
their/there

Questions involving **alphabetical ordering**:

3 Put the letters of VAUXHALL in alphabetical order.
The items in **verbal ability** tests usually take on a
limited number of forms. AAHLLUVX

Meaning of words/synonyms

4 Enormous means (the same as)
small huge normal enlarged

Unspecified relationship

5 Water is to glass as clothes are to
shop wool hangar wardrobe
(because a glass contains water, so a wardrobe
contains clothes)

Opposites

6 The opposite of knowledgeable is
uneducated ignorant intelligent intuitive coarse

Odd one out

7 Which is the odd one out?
candle coal wood heat kindling

Critical reasoning is the ability to use logical argument.

It tests whether you are able to draw inferences and conclusions from arguments and data.

8   Drive is to car as fly is to
       ship (bird) aeroplane   cycle   float   jump
       (*Source: GRT2, Psytech*)

9   Dark means the opposite of
       gloomy   happy   red   heavy (light)day
       (*Source: GRT2, Psytech*)

Verbal critical reasoning tests are often based around passages of text or sentences, and questions are then asked about them.

10 'We need to save time getting there so we'd better go by plane.'
      Is the assumption that follows taken for granted?
      'Travel by plane is more convenient than travel by train.'
      (Answer is NO. This assumption is not made in the statement as the statement is about saving time and has nothing to do with convenience.
      (*Source: Watson Glaser*)

Numerical ability

What is numerical ability?
This is the ability to work with numbers. To a great extent this is looking at attainment – that is those things that you have learnt to do over a lifetime of schooling and education. Indeed, some tests look at some very specific learnt skills, and are really tests of attainment.

However, the aptitude tests are looking at your ability to

work with numerical concepts and should not be too influenced by how much you did or did not learn at school/college/university. It is not necessarily the same as the ability to be good at mathematics, which requires a whole range of other skills as well as substantial knowledge of particular mathematical concepts. This is good news for many people, as 'mathophobia' is very common, and many people feel that they did not do justice to themselves in maths at school.

On the whole, you should be able to score well in aptitude tests without having reached a high level of attainment in formal education in maths.

However, in this section, we will look at the full range of abilities – both the more important aspects of crystallised ability (attainment) and at more fluid ability measured by the aptitude tests.

What are numerical ability tests used for?
Fairly obviously, any job which requires a knowledge and facility with numbers. This includes many clerical positions, jobs where there is a need to work with cash, and any job in finance or where you have to deal with financial information, such as budgets and accounts, or quantitative figures, such as sales figures.

Attainment
Some jobs require particular routines or arithmetic processes, and many of these can be learnt. That means that they can also be tested for. Examples would include:

- Ability to perform basic calculations or operations.
- Knowledge of basic arithmetic processes such as estimating quantities, or calculating percentages.

Aptitude testing
This relies less on particular arithmetical operations and more on the ability to spot relationships and work with numbers.

Typical questions follow below.

? **Test Yourself**

Series

1 What is the next number?
   2   4   6   8   10   ~~12~~

Relationships

2 3 is to 12 as 8 is to
   16   24   20   64   32   36
   (*Source: Psytech*)

Basic calculations

3 If £1 buys 9 francs how much will you get for £20?
   90   160   180   1800   900   209

Numerical critical reasoning
This involves drawing conclusions from numerical information, which is usually presented in the form of a table.

EXAMPLE TABLE (WOMEN)					
% of Women, within each Age Group, citing each Characteristic as the most important feature of a car.					
CHARACTERISTIC	20–29	30–39	40–49	50–59	60–69
Performance	18	12	8	10	5
Economy	17	24	29	28	32
Reliability	34	32	24	27	35
Safety	18	30	32	31	27
Design	13	2	7	4	1

(*Source: CRTB, Psytech*)

4 For women, which is the least important feature of a car?

performance   economy   reliability   safety

design   cannot say

Abstract or diagrammatic ability

What is it used for?

In fact, this category splits into two sub-categories. The first is aimed at perceptual or abstract reasoning. That is, the ability to spot patterns and logical relationships using diagrams.

The second looks at spatial ability – the ability to manipulate and understand three-dimensional objects in your head. This latter is really only relevant where people need to visualise real objects and manipulate those images. Engineering and architecture are the obvious examples. Others would include draughtsmen, and any creative visual job such as graphic design. This is obviously quite specialised.

From our point of view the former type is more important. This is because it represents our ability to think abstractly. The abstract together with the verbal and the numerical are seen as the major components of underlying fluid intelligence. Abstract ability itself is seen as important in those jobs where people have to work with complex data, with ideas and concepts. Most scientific and technical jobs come into this category.

Typical items

Although there is a large variety of items used, most of them take a similar form. This involves spotting a pattern or rule in a set of diagrams, such that you have to guess the next one in the sequence.

Here are some typical examples.

? Test Yourself

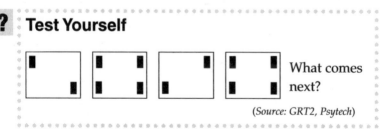

What comes next?

(*Source: GRT2, Psytech*)

For **spatial ability** it is necessary to visualise three-dimensional shapes from two-dimensional diagrams. A good way for you to check this for yourself is to imagine a three-dimensional cube. If the whole surface was painted, say red, how many faces (sides) are painted red?

As we mentioned earlier, for all of these categories of

aptitude and ability, you can increase your facility and your confidence by practising. You can turn to the practice section at the back and try some out for yourself. When you gain confidence, try to invent questions and exercises for yourself. You will see how quickly you can improve.

Summary

In this chapter we have looked at the range of aptitude and ability, and we have identified various categories within that range. We have described in detail how the three most used categories of

- verbal
- numerical
- abstract

are tested in occupational contexts. We have explained what each is most used for, and we have set out the kinds of typical questions that are used in commercial tests.

Now we go on to describe in more detail the features and characteristics of the tests themselves.

Testing aptitude and ability

As we mentioned at the beginning of this book, among the two most important questions that people ask about tests of aptitude are:

- What do they look like?
- How do I measure up?

We will look at the first of these two questions in this chapter, and at the second one in the next chapter.

Testing for aptitude and ability

Aptitude and ability are tested differently to some of the topics in the other books in this series. This is because they are invariably tested by psychometric test. Here we explain what we mean by a psychometric test, and how aptitude and ability are different, even from other kinds of psychometric tests.

What are psychometric tests? The British Psychological Society describes a psychometric test as 'an instrument designed to produce a quantitative assessment of some psychological attribute or attributes'. For the most part 'an instrument' means a paper and pencil test involving a series of multiple-choice questions.

One of the keys to the success and the wide usage of psychometric tests is that they are objective. This objectivity comes about because the tests have certain characteristics in common. Good tests should have the following characteristics:

Standardised. This means that your score should be compared to those of a 'normal' group. Any score you get should tell you how you performed in relation to the average for the compared group. This is often expressed in special measures (like percentiles or sten scores). However, what you most need to know is how you compare with the average for the group as a whole.

Reliable. They should give scores in a consistent way so that your score is independent of factors like when and where you take the test. The conditions in which the tests are administered is standardised. This includes the instructions that are given to the candidates.

Valid. They should measure a psychologically coherent attribute – ie they should measure what they say they measure. With tests of aptitude and ability this means either they should tell you something valid about a general ability, or the specific ability relates closely to real performance in the job (this is called the predictive value).

Fair. They should give equal opportunity to all people to score accurately against the attribute tested.

These principles apply to all psychometric tests. This includes tests of personality, and other measures of typical performance, as well as the tests of maximum performance such as aptitude and ability. However, from the point of view of the test-taker, there is a big difference between these two. Here are some of the differences.

Personality tests

- These are self-assessed – the answers are opinions and

judgements – what we think about ourselves. We call
these preferences.
- They are not timed.
- There are no right or wrong answers, and therefore there
are no right or wrong profiles.

Aptitude and ability tests

- They are objective – they are not based on opinion or
judgement.
- There are right answers – and wrong answers.
- They tend to be timed, to ensure accurate comparison
between test-takers.

Testing style

For aptitude and ability tests, by far the most common are
the type that involve paper and pen tests involving
multiple-choice test items with right and wrong answers.
That is because, on the whole, it is the cognitive skills that
are of most interest in testing aptitude and ability. There
can be exceptions to this, of course. Some of the more
physical and sensory-motor skills can be important in some
specialised jobs. In these cases, there are available a range of
practical tests. Tests of hand–eye coordination would be a
good example.

Other methods of testing

In this book we are focusing mostly on those aspects of
aptitude and ability that can be tested by psychometric
tests. However, they are not the only method used to test

ability. Below we outline very briefly just some of the alternative methods that can be used.

Work sample tests – these are tests designed around performance of real but representative job tasks. They tend to be used for relatively simple jobs where the individual tasks can be easily identified and specified. They are useful because of their obvious relevance, but they can be expensive and time consuming. They also need experienced and trained people to administer them.

Assessment centres – these are events organised around a range of activities that are designed to provide quality information about all relevant aspects of the participants' abilities and skills. They may include the use of standard psychometric tests, but they also generate data about underlying abilities via observed behaviour in individual and group activities, case studies, etc. They are used for external recruitment and for internal promotion and development. Their advantage is that they can be designed to elicit the relevant information very accurately, and that they are based on real behaviour. The disadvantage is that they are expensive and time consuming.

Competence-based interviews – these are structured interviews that are designed to find out about your knowledge, skills and effectiveness, in relation to defined job competencies. This is done by focusing on your experience, approach and achievements in real working contexts. Although they require a good deal of expertise to administer, they do not have the level of detail in terms of underlying aptitude, or the objectivity of psychometric tests. They are becoming increasingly popular.

360 degree appraisal – this is a means of collecting information about your performance from key stakeholders. This can include subordinates, line managers, colleagues, customers. It should be structured against relevant competencies, and should be based on observed behaviour rather than subjective judgement. To obtain this kind of quality information requires substantial resources, including time and expertise to administer. Also, it doesn't replace information about underlying aptitude and ability, as it focuses on how this manifests in behaviour in the real working environment.

As you can see from the above, many of these techniques (and others) are aimed at providing high-quality information, and most of them can deliver on that promise. However, in and of themselves, they don't provide information that replaces objective psychometric information, but supplement it. It is for this reason that many of these are used in conjunction with, rather than in replacement of, tests of aptitude and ability.

Some tests that you might use

Below we will describe some of the most common tests that are used by professional psychologists and HR departments. The purpose of this is to give you an idea, in broad terms, of what you might expect. It should also help you understand some of the commonalities and the differences between such tests.

It is not the purpose of this section for you to be able to 'mug up' on each of these tests, to gain an unfair advantage over others who might take the tests with you. This would benefit no-one. It wouldn't benefit the publisher because it could 'contaminate' the tests, thus reducing their effectiveness and objectivity. It wouldn't benefit the organisation because it could lead to poor or flawed decision-making. And finally, and most importantly, it wouldn't benefit you. This is because, in the last analysis, there is not much point in misrepresenting your aptitudes and abilities to a potential or real employer. This might lead you to be employed or promoted into a position for which you are not suited, and thus cause stress or unhappiness. Alternatively, it could lead to development being diagnosed or delivered wrongly for you. Our main objective, therefore, is to provide information that will help to allay anxiety.

In fact, it is not unusual these days for test publishers to provide test-takers with practice papers. This is precisely because they want you to know what you are being asked to do, but also want to preserve the fairness and objectivity of the actual tests.

It is worth pointing out that test publishers often collect together series of tests that test related aptitudes. These are called test batteries. Batteries of two, three, or even ten related tests are quite common, as you will see from the descriptions below.

The sections below are basic descriptions. Although we add comments, these should not be taken for professional evaluations of the tests or test batteries. If you would like to see such a thing, the British Psychological Society does provide objective evaluations for professional users.

We have divided tests and test batteries up by the level of the job to which they tend to be applied.

General intelligence tests

As we have emphasised elsewhere, these are used less and less these days, having been replaced, on the whole, by more specific and specialised tests. However, the most famous and well used of those available is:

Ravens Progressive Matrices

Provider: The Test Agency.

Format: SPM is 60 problems in five sets of 12.
APM is 36 problems.

If they are timed, the time limit is 40 minutes.

They say: 'The Standard and Advanced Progressive Matrices are designed to assess a person's intellectual and reasoning ability. The Advanced test is designed for people of above average intellectual capability ... and provides a means of assessing all the analytical and integral operations involved in higher thought processes.'

Level: SPM is the standard set for general purposes, and APM is the more advanced set for graduate and managerial.

Covering: Intellectual and reasoning ability. They are non-verbal and comprise sets of sequences of symbolic (visual) figures, of which you have to find the next in the sequence.

Comment: As the name implies, they are progressive – that is they get harder as you go along. Unusual, in that they are not always timed. The timing adds the dimension about efficiency as well as capacity.

Basic tests of aptitude and ability

Employment Aptitude Survey (EAS)

Provider: The Test Agency.

Format: 10 × five-minute tests.

They say: 'A battery of aptitude measures designed for the selection of applicants at all levels ... is also ideal for apprenticeship selection and general guidance.'

Level: All levels, including secretarial, clerical, retail, technical sales.

Covering: A range of aptitudes:

- verbal comprehension
- numerical ability
- visual pursuit
- visual speed and accuracy
- spatial visualisation
- numerical reasoning
- verbal reasoning
- word fluency
- manual speed and accuracy
- symbolic reasoning.

Comments: A very wide range covered, not all of which will be useful or needed in many real applications.

Automated Office Battery

Provider: Saville and Holdsworth.

Format: Three tests of 10, 12 and 18 minutes.

They say: ' ... identifies the skills needed to work in an automated office environment'.

Level: General education level, or basic to good GCSE, covering such as accounts clerks, mail order operatives, anyone working a VDU.

Covering: Numerical estimating, computer checking, coded instructions.

Comments: Quite specialised, and for use for those working in an automated office environment. Used for school leavers and work-experience applicants.

General Reasoning Test (GRT2)

Provider: Psytech.

Format: Two tests of 10 minutes and one of eight minutes.

They say: 'A comprehensive, detailed and accurate measure of mental ability, this test has been designed to assess reasoning power for those of general ability.'

Level: General education level, a wide range of abilities and applications.

Covering: Verbal, numerical and abstract reasoning.

Comments: Focused on mental ability rather than any specific attainments. Assesses the minimum level needed for many jobs.

Graduate and managerial tests

We should make the point that many of the general tests above can be appropriate for graduate and managerial level positions. However, there are some test batteries that focus particularly on this group. Here are some typical ones.

Graduate Reasoning Test (GRT1)

Provider: Psytech.

Format: Two tests of 10 minutes and one of eight minutes.

They say: 'The test has been designed to assess high-level reasoning ability.'

Level: Graduate and managerial.

Covering: Verbal, numerical and abstract reasoning.

Comments: Designed to assess people of graduate ability, it only needs a general level of ability to complete. So it can be used to identify people with potential for development or progression.

Advance Managerial Tests (AMT)

Provider: Saville and Holdsworth.

Format: A series of tests ranging from 20 minutes to 35 minutes.

They say: ' ... the tests are designed to assess ... across a range of functions.'

Level: Managers, professional and graduates.

Covering: Verbal application, verbal analysis, numerical reasoning, numerical analysis.

Comments: Mixes understanding of meaning of words, interpreting of complex verbal information, interpreting complex numerical data and numerical reasoning. Calculators are allowed, which emphasises that it is the reasoning, rather than the operational or computational skill, that is being tested.

Critical reasoning tests

Critical Reasoning Test Battery (CRTB)

Provider: Psytech.

Format: Two tests, of 20 minutes and 30 minutes.

They say: 'A detailed and accurate measure of critical reasoning ... they can be used to assess general ability and to identify particular areas of strength and weakness.'

Level: Graduate and management.

Covering: Verbal critical reasoning and numerical critical reasoning.

Comments: Used to identify management potential, for graduate recruitment, and senior management assessment.

Watson Glaser Critical Thinking Appraisal

Provider: The Test Agency or Oxford Psychologist Press.

Format: 80 items in five sections. Takes 40 minutes if
timed.

They say: 'This battery measures five aspects of the ability
to think critically.'

Level: Graduate and management.

Covering:

- drawing inferences from facts
- recognising assumptions
- reasoning by deduction
- reasoning by interpretation
- discriminating strong and weak
  arguments.

Comments: Can be timed or untimed. Applicable across a
wide range of higher level jobs.

Trends

Finally, it should be pointed out that the way organisations
are using tests has changed over the years, and continues to
change. Here are some trends that you may be affected by,
or that you may notice.

Job-related validity

There has been some scepticism about the validity of data
provided by test suppliers. Organisations themselves are

becoming more sophisticated in terms of job analysis and in understanding the criteria that indicate success in their own organisations. They therefore look for tests that relate to job-related criteria.

Specific aptitudes

Along with the trend described above, there has been a move away from general tests (particularly of IQ) towards the testing of more specific aptitudes.

'Friendliness' of tests

A test is a test, but efforts have been made to make tests appear more relevant to real working life (face validity), as well as to present them in a less formidable and possibly anxiety creating way. Many commercial test producers now offer 'practice' papers that allow the test-takers to understand beforehand the format, and the kinds of questions that will be asked. Many of the newer tests are also much shorter.

Fairness

A good deal of effort has been expended to make tests culture fair. That is, no person taking a test should be disadvantaged by virtue of their gender or cultural background.

Summary

In this chapter, we have described the key features of psychometric tests in general and, in particular, how tests of ability and aptitude differ from other psychometric tests, such as tests of personality. We have also described some of the more common and typical commercial tests that you might face. Finally, we have described some trends in test-taking that might affect you.

At this stage it would now be useful to find your 'base level' of aptitude and ability. The next section is a series of tests and exercises that will provide you with this information.

Testing your own aptitude and ability

So far, we have mainly *talked about* aptitude and ability. Now we need to move on and show you how to assess your own aptitude and ability. We shall do this in two parts. These are:

- Evaluating your ability
- The ability tests

The second part, and the bulk of this chapter will be a series of tests to give you some objective information. For many of you, who have been or are likely to be tested in real situations, it is important to have this information.

However, it is not the only way to evaluate your abilities and achievements in life. Many people forget (including, unfortunately, many HR practitioners and professionals) that there already exists a good deal of quality information about these aspects of your talents. Most experienced working people have a lifetime of learning and achievement behind them. This all provides an idea or indication of your aptitude and ability.

Evaluating your ability

Let's start with a simple set of questions. You have now read about aptitude and ability – what it is and what it comprises. If we focus mainly on cognitive (mental) abilities, think about the following.

Compared to the rest of the population, how would you rate your:

	Above average	Average	Below average
Verbal ability			
Numerical ability			
Abstract reasoning			

- What other known strengths do you have?
- Are there any known weaknesses or 'blind spots'?
- Are there any other distinct abilities you know you have?

That's not a bad overall picture. For most testing purposes, that is exactly the kind of judgement that they are looking for. The only difference is that they are likely to put numbers to those kinds of comparisons, as well as objectivity to the means of testing.

You should remember that for most people, they are not equally comfortable or talented with each of these categories. We all have our strengths and weaknesses.

That leads us on, though, to ask:

- How do you know you are right?
- What kind of information or evidence did you use?

For instance, have you got any objective or third-party information to balance your own opinion? For most of us, there is a great deal of information in the system. These are some of the things that you might ask yourself.

Was your formal education:

- Up to 16 (GCSE)
- Up to 18 (A level, BTEC, GNVQ, Baccalaureate)
- Higher education (University, HE College)
- Postgraduate

For each of the last three, you are likely to be progressively higher than average in your chosen subject areas.

List your qualifications – all of your qualifications, including vocational ones. What is the highest grade or level at which you studied: language/literature/ communication and a mathematical or numerate subject?

What, now, about your experience and achievements at work? What do they tell you about your abilities and preferences?

Finally, in each of the three categories we are focusing on, if you were asked to justify or 'prove' your ability, what evidence (including answers to the questions above) could you offer to convince someone of that ability. You can include any positive feedback you have had on any of these aspects of your ability.

Finally, revisit your assessment, in the light of this evidence.

	Above average	Average	Below average	Reason/ evidence
Verbal ability				
Numerical ability				
Abstract reasoning				

Now, let's look at some objective evidence to complete the picture. You will find the answers on pages 87–90.

The ability tests

Verbal ability

Set 1

We will start with a set of questions that will give you an idea of your learnt abilities (attainment) in the verbal field. (*Time guide – eight minutes.*)

? **Test Yourself**

Choose the correct spelling for each:

1 a) acsept b) acept c) accept d) accsept
2 a) diseeve b) deceive c) decieve d) deseive
3 a) parrallel b) paralell c) parralel d) parallel
4 a) unnecessary b) unecesary c) unnesesary
   d) unecesary
5 a) releeved b) releived c) relived d) relieved

Put these in alphabetical order:

6 The letters of RHOMBUS BHMORSU
7 CASTLE CATT CASTOR CATTELL CASSADY
8 POULSON POINTON POROBIC POWELL
   PORTER

Which word means the same as:

9 START a) open b) begin c) stop d) grow
10 BEFORE a) precedence b) first c) preceding
    d) antecedant

cassidy , Castle , Castor , CATT , CATTELL
POINTON ~~Porto~~. Porobic , Porter , Poulson Powel

11 ESCORT a) accompany b) guide c) carry d) take

Which word means the opposite of:

12 LOVE a) dislike b) disdain c) disparage d) hate

13 FIND a) discover b) lose c) mislay d) retrieve

Complete the sentence:

14 The children forgot to take _their_ lunch to school.

their/there

15 The pain was almost too much to _bear_.

bear/bare

Set 2

These questions should help you to assess your underlying verbal ability, or aptitude. (*Time guide – five minutes.*)

?

Test Yourself

Which is the odd one out:

1 a) hammer b) screwdriver c) scissors d) nail

2 a) box b) paper c) jug d) envelope e) bag

3 a) sparrow b) terrier c) deer d) tabby

4 a) bright b) green c) happy d) painting

5 a) order b) obey c) instruct d) tell

Complete the equations:

6 question is to ask as story is to

a) say b) book c) tell d) listen

7 wheel is to car as wing is to

a) aeroplane b) nut c) feather d) flat

8 kitten is to cat as cub is to
   a) young b) dog c) lion d) animal

9 cold is to freeze as warm is to
   a) hot b) boil c) scolding d) temperature

10 head is to hat as hand is to
   a) arm b) finger c) hold d) glove

Set 3

These questions test your verbal critical reasoning. (*Time guide – three minutes.*)

? Test Yourself

'Most swans are white. All white swans are aggressive.'

Decide whether the following two statements are:
a) definitely true b) definitely false c) can't tell

1 All swans are aggressive. (a)
2 If a swan is aggressive it must be white. (b)

'The foreign secretary argues that the deal is the country's best chance for peace. Assuming that the deal does not collapse, the amnesty will be agreed and the question of bringing the criminals before the tribunal does not arise.'

For each of the following statements, decide whether it is:
a) definitely true b) probably true c) can't tell
d) probably false e) definitely false

3 Peace is assured. (e)
4 The criminals will not be brought to the tribunal. (c)
5 The deal won't collapse. (c)

Numerical Ability

Set 1

Again, the first set of questions will test your learnt ability (attainment) of basic arithmetic processes. They should be answered without using a calculator. Aim to do them as quickly as possible (*Time guide – 10 minutes.*)

?

Test Yourself

1 26 + 15 (41)   **2** 9 + 17 (26)   **3** 14 + 13 (27)

4 36 + 28 (64)   **5** 11 − 7 (4)   **6** 22 − 9 (11)

7 35 − 7 (28)   **8** 44 − 18 (26)   **9** 7 × 12 (84)

10 9 × 15 (135)   **11** 4 × 26 (104)   **12** 2 × 49 (98)

13 35 ÷ 5 (7)   **14** 84 ÷ 4 (21)   **15** 75 ÷ 15 (5)

16 105 ÷ 7 (15)   **17** 1.6 + 3.9 (5.4)   **18** 15.2 − 1.8 (13.4)

19 2.5 × 6 (15.0)   **20** 7.5 ÷ 3 (2.13)   **21** ½ + ¼ (2.6)

22 ⁷⁄₁₀ − ½ ⁵⁄₉   **23** ⅔ × 2 (4.6)   **24** 2½ ÷ ½ (1/6)

25 10% of £2 (20p)   **26** 25% of £3.60 (90)   **27** 5% of £58 £2.40

28 50% of £7.36 £3.70

29 A shelf holds 45 tins of fruit and there are eight shelves. How many tins is this? 440

30 I have book tokens for £20, if I use them to buy books worth £5.99 and £8.50, how much change should I receive? £5.51

nos – 21, 22, 23, 24

P 82-90

Set 2

These questions should help you to assess your numerical aptitude, or ability to reason with numbers. (*Time guide – eight minutes.*)

? **Test Yourself**

Find the next term in the sequence:

1 1   4   7   10   13   _16_ ✓

2 15   13   11   9   7   _5_ ✓

3 2   6   18   54   _162_ ✓

4 1   3   7   15   ~~31~~ ✓
 (handwritten: 2 4 8 16)

5 1   1   2   3   5   8   ____

6 5 is to 15 as 7 is to ___
   a) 14   b) 75   (c) 21)   d) 27 ✓

7 45% is to 100% as 9 is to
   a) 20   (b) 5)   c) 45   d) 10 ✗

8 ⅖ is to 0.4 as ⁷⁄₁₀ is to
   a) 7   (b) 0.8)   c) 0.7   d) 1.4 ✗

9 40% is to 2\5 as 75% is to
   a) ⅜   b) ¼   c) ⅚   d) ¾ ✗

10 27 is to 22 as 14 is to ?
   (a) 9)   b) 12   c) 10   (d) 17) ✗ *answer is a*

11 Which is the odd one out?
   a) 3   b) 12   c) 15   d) 18   (e) 10) ✓

54

12 There are 9 francs to the £1, how many francs for £17?

a) 1.88   b) 90   c) 153   d) 189

13 A campsite costs £7.50 per night. How much for a week?

a) £56   b) £37.50   c) £49   d) £52.50

14 Florida is five hours behind London time. A flight leaves London at 1000 and takes eight hours. What time (local) does it arrive in Florida?

a) 1300   b) 2300   c) 1800   d) 1500

15 I have £225 left to pay on a loan, which is paid at £15 a month. How many months left to pay?

a) 12   b) 15   c) 10   d) 18

Set 3

This set of questions tests your numerical critical reasoning. (*Time guide – five minutes.*)

? Test Yourself

In a poll, some members of the general public were shown a range of sentences for various crimes and asked to indicate the sentence they thought most appropriate to the crime. Their choices are shown in the table.

	% OF RESPONDENTS			
	1–3 years prison	Less than one year in prison	Fine	Probation
Burglary	25	15	23	/
Vandalism	17	17	16	11
Shoplifting	7	8	57	17
Confidence tricks	42	17	20	/

1 For which crime do people most want custodial *Confidence* ⟶
   sentences?

2 Which crime do people seem to think is the least *Vandalism*
   serious?

3 More people prefer custodial sentences for vandalism.
   True or false? *False* ✓

Four teams, Alton, Barford, Camdown and Desworth
played each other once in a football league (three points
for a win, one for a draw).

Barford were the only team not to win a game. *Lost*
Each team drew once.
Alton won most games. *won*
Nobody won all of their games.

4 How many points did Alton get? 4

5 How many did Camdown get? 4

Abstract ability

This set of questions tests your abstract reasoning. (Time
guide – eight minutes.)

?

Test Yourself

What comes next in each sequence?

1 ○   △   □   ○   △   □   ○

2 ●   ◉   ○   ●   ◉   ?   ○

3 ↑   →   ↓   ?   ←

— 56 —

4 'l   l'   l.   ?   ⸮   .l

5 **X I X**   **X X I**   **I X X**   **? ✕ I ✕**

6 ⌐ ⊔ L ⌐ □ ⌐   ?

7 **O O T O T**   **T O O T O**   **O T O O T**   ?

8 Which is the odd one out?

   a) [⋰ . ⋰]   b) [∷ .]   c) [□ ∷]   d) [∷ .]

9 Which is the odd one out?

   a) o⊢—+   b) —⊣o⁺   c) �   d) ⌇⁺

10 ↑ is to → as ↓ is to ? ⇐

11 ◺ is to ◿ as ◿ is to ? ◹

12 **a** is to **BB** as **e** is to ? FF

13 ⌐ is to L as ⌐ is to ? |⁻

14 **BAAB** is to **ABBA** as **TXXT** is to ? TTXX

15 **BCD** is to **EDC** as **FGH** is to ? IGH

If you now turn to the next chapter, you can score up your test, and find out how to interpret your test scores.

Interpreting your test scores

In this section we will look at ways of making sense of your test scores and interpreting them. To do this we will look at:

- How scores are standardised
- Rating your scores
- Using your test assessment

How scores are standardised

Before we turn to your own test scores, we should explain how scores are used and interpreted when real, commercial tests are used. Most people, when they take any kind of test, are interested to know what their 'score' is. There are two underlying assumptions here that are common to most people. These are:

1. The result will be a single number or score.
2. That the score is just the number of right answers, perhaps expressed as a percentage.

In fact, both of these assumptions tend to be wrong. Of course, as we have pointed out previously, aptitude and ability tests are based on right and wrong answers, but it is not the number of right answers that is the most important thing. As we have also described, what is important about these tests is that the scores are standardised. What this means is that your scores are compared to those of a known group of people. Distributions of scores for a known group of people are called norms. The known group of people itself might be the general population, graduates, managers, people in a particular organisation, etc.

The standardisation works in the following way. When you have a group of people take a test, the scores will be distributed from low to high. Invariably, these scores, when graphed, will look like this:

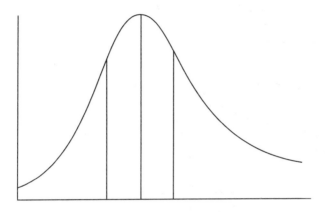

This is called the normal (or 'bell') curve and is very common for many naturally occuring measures. What happens then is that this distribution is 'carved up' into segments. These segments can be based on numbers. So, if the distribution is carved into hundredths, they are called percentiles. If it is carved into ten, they are called sten (or standard tens) scores. Your score, then, is not given as a raw score (such as 25 out of 40, for instance). Your score is compared to the distribution. If percentiles are used, the 80th percentile does not mean you scored 80%, but that you scored more than 80% of the norm population. In other words, the feedback is comparing your performance to that of the rest of the normed group.

In many cases, this is not even done by numbers, but by banding or slicing the distribution into categories (as shown in the diagram above). So quite often, the feedback you get will not be in the form of a number, but might be in the form of a statement like:

- 'in the top band'
- 'average'
- 'as well as most people . . .'

and other similar statements.

If you think about the first section of the last chapter, where we asked you to evaluate your own aptitude and ability, if you could be reasonably sure you are 'above average', 'average', or 'below average', this is all the information you need.

In terms of the tests we present in this book, they have not been standardised. We have suggested that the scores are placed in bands (low, medium and high) which will give you a fair indication, but not an exact comparison to a known group. For that, you would have to complete a commercial test.

Rating your scores

The first thing you need to do is to score up your tests. The correct answers can be found on pages 87–90.

When looking at your overall scores, there are a number of things to bear in mind.

1 The scores make more sense if you followed the time guidelines. Time is an important factor. If you, for instance, answered all of the numerical questions right, but it took you an hour to do it, that is different to getting them all right within the time guidelines. The time gives a measure, not just of the accuracy, but of the fluency with which you can reason with (in this case) numbers. However, it can be useful to know that you are accurate, even if you are slow.

2 These scores are not standardised. That means we can't compare you to a known population, such as the general population. So the benchmark information we are providing below is rating your performance against the tasks in hand. However, because these tests are fairly similar and typical, they are very much 'in the style of' and comparable to commercially available tests that you might be asked to do. Therefore, your scores should give a good indication as to how well you would do in a 'real' test, with standardised scores.

These benchmarks should provide you with a good idea of your actual and potential performance.

Verbal ability

Set 1
The scores are out of 15, so:

0–7	8–11	12–15
low	medium	high

It is worth pointing out that we have sampled here some of the key areas of verbal attainment, which should give an idea as to your overall level of attainment. Some jobs, and therefore some tests will test for more specific aspects of attainment (an example will be ability to deal with detail), which is not covered by this test.

Sets 2 and 3
The scores are out of 10 and 5, making 15 in all, so:

0–7	8–11	12–15
low	medium	high

The 'hardest' questions to answer are likely to be the five critical reasoning questions, so it is worth paying attention to your score in this subset, because there are tests that focus solely on critical reasoning.

Numerical ability

Set 1
This is a measure of how well you have learnt and remembered some of the basic operations you were taught at school. The scores are out of 30, so:

0–15	16–23	24–30
low	medium	high

Sets 2 and 3
These are scored out of 15 and 5, making 20 in all, so:

0–10	11–15	16–20
low	medium	high

Again, it is also worth looking separately at how well you did in the numerical critical reasoning in its own right.

Abstract ability

These were scored out of 15, so:

0–7	8–11	12–15
low	medium	high

Putting the picture together

Now you have all the scores, you should be able to see the overall pattern.

	Low	Medium	High
Verbal attainment			✓
Verbal reasoning	✓		
Numerical attainment		✓	
Numerical reasoning		✓	
Abstract		✓	

Enter your ratings with a tick in this table. This should provide a total picture.

Within this, you can ask yourself some questions. Some useful considerations include:

- How did I do overall?
- Which are my strongest and weakest areas?
- Do these scores correspond with my own assessment of my strengths and weaknesses?
- Do they relate to my performance at work, or the job and career choices I have made?

- Is there a difference between my attainment and ability scores? How might this have come about?

A further question, of course, is:

What can I do about it?

For some people, their aptitude scores are below their expectations, or below their apparent level of attainment in their job. As a typical example, people often say: 'How can my numerical aptitude be low when I use spreadsheets for my budgeting perfectly well?'

There can be a number of factors involved in such situations. It is quite possible that a person's basic aptitude is not that high, but their achievement is higher than this alone would suggest. Some people can be accurate but slow – perhaps lacking some fluidity with this type of data. This does not mean that they cannot learn to manipulate (in this case) numbers with some skill. This is a triumph of attainment, learning and application.

It is important that people understand that scores rarely mean 'can't'. This also provides some ideas to the question posed above. To put it in a nutshell, you may have to work harder, but most people can learn the skills they need if their motivation is high enough, and they have identified what skills it is they need to learn.

Using your test assessment

For many people, the time to do this type of assessment is

when they are thinking about career change or development. This can mean either applying for jobs, or seeking new roles or progression with one's current employer. For some, it means a complete evaluation of career choices and options altogether.

This means it makes sense to think of our results in terms of career choices. A good way to think about career themes is to use one of the accepted career classification schemes. We use the one based on the work of Holland, although there are many of these schemes and classifications about.

The advantage of such a scheme is that it can help to give us a match between our profiles and those of the broad occupational groups referred to below.

Career theme scales

Realistic theme. Based on activity and direct involvement in tasks, particularly physical tasks. Preferences include use of equipment and mechanical devices, technical disciplines, outdoor activity.

Investigative theme. Based on the manipulation of ideas and scientific principles. Preferences include scientific, logical and experimental work.

Artistic theme. Based on use of artistic and creative faculties. Preferences include the arts in all of its guises, such as media, music, writing, design and so on.

Social theme. Based on person-centred interests, including caring, people-vocational. Preferences include caring for and helping others, counselling, teaching.

Enterprising theme. Based on leadership and management, achievement and control. Preferences include business and business development.

Conventional theme. Based on organising, administering and working with procedures and systems. Preferences range from clerical and administration to accountancy, business systems and quality compliance functions.

Clearly, some of these require different aptitudes and abilities, and our own repertoire of aptitudes and abilities will influence our interest in these themes.

Most of us we don't have just one single exclusive interest in the themes in this list. However, we will have preferences. Try for yourself by rating your interest in each one. Rate your interest as high, medium or low.

	high	medium	low
Realistic			
Investigative			
Artistic			
Social			
Enterprising			
Conventional			

Remember that this is our interest and preferences that we are rating, and that this should show a profile across these themes. So it is perfectly possible that you rate more than one of these as high.

Can you see any patterns in your responses?

Remember, also, that any individual job or career may also relate to these in subtle ways. For instance, it would be quite easy to see that certain jobs in a customer service environment might involve a mixture of realistic and social.

What kinds of jobs might be implied by the mixture of your own high ratings?

We should also point out that interest will relate to our personal preferences and typical performance behaviour. This can be studied more in the *Test Your Personality* book in this series.

Another factor in addition to the interest factor is the ability factor. Each of these may require different abilities to support competence in that particular area. Again, to take an example, what kind of abilities do you think you would need to be good at jobs and careers with a high social theme?

Many of the skills will be interpersonal skills and communication skills. You are likely to learn more about these in relation to tests of personality. In this particular case, your emotional intelligence (EQ) might be more relevant. (Again, if you are interested in this, read the forthcoming *Test Your Emotional Intelligence* book in this series.)

Although it is not an exact science, you might want to try and guess how each of these relate to the three basic abilities we have been using.

How does this now relate to your own profile of abilities from your own evaluation and from the testing you have done? You will need to make an evaluation on your spatial, mechanical and clerical/checking based on the best information you have.

How does this profile relate to your current job role, and to your planned ambitions?

Summary

Now you have scored up your tests, we shall move on to look at what you can do to develop your own skills.

Developing your aptitude and ability

In this final chapter, we shall be looking at how you can prepare yourself for the process of testing, and how you can help develop your own aptitude and ability. To do this we will look at:

- Preparing for testing
- Developing your ability
- Practice

Preparing for testing

One important way in which you can develop yourself in relation to aptitude and ability testing is to make sure that you perform to the best of your ability in a real testing situation. For many people, ignorance of the process and anxiety during the testing mean that they do not perform to their full potential.

The testing process

The first thing you should be aware of is what to expect in the testing process itself. Here are a few simple guidelines for the steps involved:

1 Familiarise yourself with the tests themselves.
  As we have already mentioned, it is quite normal for test publishers to provide practice and familiarisation material. Don't be afraid to ask for this if it is not provided automatically. Failing that, you are entitled to ask about the nature of the test – what kinds of test; what

it/they comprise; if there are any descriptions or guidelines, and so on.

2 Find out about the arrangements.
   This should include the obvious and basic considerations such as the start time and the location. You should also be forewarned of the duration of the test(s) themselves. Check if there are any special considerations or if you need to bring any equipment. (You shouldn't need to, but checking is always a reassurance.)

3 The testing.
   The testing itself should be done in an environment that is conducive. That is, it should be comfortable, and it should be free from disturbance. To aid standardisation, all candidates should do the testing in the same conditions, preferably at the same time. There should be a trained and qualified test administrator. He/she should:

   • provide the appropriate materials
   • describe the context, purpose and process
   • read the instructions
   • invigilate the test (including timing if appropriate)
   • arrange for the scoring to be done.

4 Feedback.
   You should always be made aware of if, how and when feedback will be given. There are circumstances where feedback is not given. This is sometimes the case, for instance, in the testing of external candidates for recruitment. However, in many cases feedback will only be given if it is requested, and so it is always worthwhile making the request. Where feedback is given, it should

be constructive and confidential. The opportunity to discuss the results should always be offered.

Preparing yourself for testing

Because testing does involve anxiety for many, you can use your preparation time as an opportunity to present yourself for the test in the best frame of mind possible. These are some ideas that might assist you in achieving that:

1 Get clued up.
   Use the opportunity to find out as much as you can about the purpose and the nature of the tests, the timings, and so on. As mentioned above, use the opportunity to ask for practice material if it is available. This way there should be no surprises on the day.

2 Familiarisation.
   Use what practice material is available (or the nearest you can find). This has two benefits. The first is to help your brain get used to thinking in the right kind of ways required for the test. The second is really about reassurance. Again, once you know what to expect, and you have 'had a go', it means that there are no unpleasant surprises, and this helps you to get the best out of yourself.

3 Manage your state of mind.
   This involves a number of elements. Certainly you should arrive at the day in the right state of mind. Make sure you have had a few good nights' sleep before the day. Relaxing activity the day/night before always helps. This is achieved in different ways by different people, but can involve exercise, leisure or

other means of relaxation. Finally, use every opportunity to give yourself positive messages. There is no doubt that if you tell yourself that you will make a mess of it, you are more than halfway to doing just that! Many people have supportive friends or loved ones who can help in this.

4 The day itself.
Time your arrival just right. Being late and flustered will not help, but neither will being there an hour before with nothing positive to do. The key is to be physically relaxed, while being mentally alert.

5 The test itself.
It is difficult to give very general advice because tests differ so much. In approach to the test, it is better to do the questions in order. You should do those that are easy to do, or at least not too difficult. In a short timed test, it is usually a mistake to spend a long time poring over a question that you may get wrong anyway. The best rule is to do as much as you can do well straight away, then use any time left to do what else you can.

Developing your ability

Developing verbal ability

Although test designers claim that they are measuring aptitude (except where they are specifically trying to measure attainment), there are some things you can do to help develop your skills and facility with words. Because verbal ability is all about the use of words, the ways of developing your ability involve:

- widening your vocabulary, and
- using that vocabulary.

Some things you can do to help:

- read quality newspapers
- read books – particularly factual ones
- do crosswords
- involve yourself in debate/discussion/argument
- when you see a new word – look it up in the dictionary
- play games – like reading a passage and trying to identify the abstract nouns.

Developing numerical skills
This involves 'getting friendly' with numbers, as well as learning and developing some very basic arithmetic routines. Once developed, practice improves not only the skill, but also the speed or fluidity with which you can perform operations. (This is the reason, of course, why most aptitude tests are timed.) This has a very positive effect on the confidence of most people – particularly those who have felt less than comfortable with maths in the past.

One of the best ways to begin to do this is to improve your mental arithmetic. This can best be done by beginning to 'play' with numbers in your head. Some ways to achieve this include:

- halving numbers in your head
- doubling numbers in your head
- getting friendly with percentages.

This can be done by understanding some basic relationships, such as 10% is the same as ⅒. You can obtain this by dividing by ten. This is usually easier in the first instance with money amounts. So 10% of £21 is ⅒ of £21. This is £2.10. Other common percentages can be found as multiples of 10%.

To find 50% just half the amount.
To find 25% just half and half again.

Practice the unfamiliar – for many people this means particularly fractions.

Developing abstract and spatial ability
Each of the two categories mentioned needs to be developed in a slightly different way.

For abstract ability:

- learn to spot patterns
- try the puzzles in popular puzzle books
- learn to memorise sets of instructions
- invent sequences of symbols (like the ones in the tests).

For spatial ability:

- practice visualising, holding and manipulating three-dimensional images
- cut out nets of cubes with patterns and see how they assemble
- handle and study solid objects closely.

As we mentioned earlier, for all of these categories of aptitude and ability, you can increase your facility and your confidence by practising. You can now have a go at the practice section and try some out for yourself. When you gain confidence, try to invent questions and exercises for yourself. You will see how quickly you can improve.

Practice

Practice makes perfect. Well, not quite! However, the brain, like any other part of the body, does improve if we use it. For many of us, some of the pathways and processes involved in aptitude and ability tests have not been much used since school. Practice can help in a number of ways:

1 *Confidence*. When we know better what we are facing, and when we know 'the rules', we can lessen our anxiety. We should also get some confidence from the feedback from doing the practice.
2 *Consolidation*. We enhance our skills by using them.
3 *Fluidity*. This is the mental 'fitness' that comes from practice and using our brains and our skills.

The format of these sections follows that of the earlier testing section. Your performance and results from that section will influence which (if any) of these sections you may need to concentrate on. Answers are provided on pages 89–90.

Verbal ability

Set 1

?

Test Yourself

Choose the correct spelling for each:

1 a) desiese b) disease c) desease d) disiese
2 a) eligible b) elligible c) eligable d) elagable
3 a) shedule b) shedyule c) schedule d) schedool
4 a) rhythm b) rithem c) rhitham d) rhythmn
5 a) questionnaire b) questionairre c) questionaire
   d) questionnairre

Put these words in alphabetical order:

6 The letters of MISTAKE   AEIKMST
7 MORANT MORRIS MORGAN MORONEY
   MOULTON
8 PRAJAPATI POWROZNYK PRAXMARER
   PREMJI POZYLO

Which word means the same as:

9 CLOSE a) imminent b) far c) near d) distant
10 FIX a) sort b) put c) add d) mend
11 MOIST a) wet b) damp c) soaking d) water

Which word means the opposite of:

12 BORROW a) give b) loan c) receive d) lend
13 LOSE a) discover b) find c) retreive d) mislay

Complete the sentence:

14 He ___has___ to complete the report by Tuesday.
   as/has
15 I'll wait here while you ___hail___ the taxi.
   hale/hail

Set 2

? ## Test Yourself

Which is the odd one out?

1 a) candle   b) coal   c) wood   d) heat

2 a) say   b) obey   c) instruct   d) order

3 a) read   b) book   c) paper   d) novel

4 a) Jersey   b) Belgium   c) Cyprus   d) Australia

5 a) dog   b) cat   c) shark   d) tiger

6 What 3-letter word can go before each of these?
   Coat   light   hot   *(Red)*

7 What 3 letters can go before each of these to make
   one word?
   bate   claim   cure

8 Here is to where as now is to
   a) when   b) time   c) then   d) never

9 Phone is to ear as TV is to
   a) picture   b) see   c) eye   d) watch

10 Book is to read as house is to
   a) kitchen   b) roof   c) brick   d) build

Set 3

? **Test Yourself**

'*All Venusians are tall. Some Venusians are not friendly.*'

Decide whether the following two statements are:

a) definitely true   b) definitely false   c) can't tell

1 Friendly Venusians are tall.
2 No Venusians are tall and friendly.

'*The white paper is full of promises to regulate rogue traders. Regulation, however – even if it does happen – will not solve the problem of poor services. Only the power of the consumers can do that.*'

For each of the following statements, decide whether it is:

a) definitely true   b) probably true   c) can't tell
d) probably false   e) definitely false
3 The government will regulate poor services. (e)
4 Consumer power can solve the problem. b
5 Regulation is a good thing. (c)

Numerical ability

Set 1

? **Test Yourself**

1 9 + 18	**2** 17 + 13	**3** 26 + 15
4 37 + 24	**5** 15 − 8	**6** 23 − 7
7 35 − 19	**8** 81 − 36	**9** 5 × 13
10 7 × 18	**11** 9 × 15	**12** 3 × 47

13 55 ÷ 5 = 11 ✓ **14** 52 ÷ 4 = 13 ✓ **15** 64 ÷ 16 4 ✓
16 138 ÷ 6 = 23 ✓ **17** 1.8 + 3.7 5.5 ✓ **18** 12.9 − 2.5 = 10.4 ✓
19 1.5 × 8 = 12.0 ✓ **20** 12.0 ÷ 1.5 ? **21** 2\3 + ½ 1⅙ ✓
22 ¾ − 7⁄10 ? **23** ⅜ × 2 **24** 1½ ÷ ¼ ?
25 10% of £5 0.50 **26** 25% of £4.40 **27** 50% of £11
28 30% of £20 £1.10 ✓ 5.50 ✓
£6.00 ✓

29 A factory uses 15 tonnes of sand per day. How much
does it use in a 20-working-day month? 300 Tonnes

30 I went out with £42 and came home with £5.50. How
much did I spend? £36.50 ✓

Set 2 Do

Test Yourself

Find the next term in each sequence:

1 3	5	7	9	11	13?
2 4	11	18	25	?	32 ✓
3 231	224	217	210	?	203 ✓
4 1.5	3	4.5	6	?	7.5 ✓
5 2	6	18	54	?	162 ✓

6 6 is to 18 as 3 is to
   a) 15   b) 6   c) 9   d)12

7 60% is to ⅗ as 25% is to
   a) ¾   b) 0.25   c) ½   d) ¼ ?

8 15 is to 9 as 20 is to
   a) 12   b) 13   c) 15   d) 11 ✓

9 2 is to 0.5 as 4 is to
   a) 0.4   b) 0.25   c) 0.2   d) 0.45 ?

10 3 and 5 are to 15 as 2 and 6 are to
   a) 26   b) 8   c) 3   d) 12 ✓

11 Which is the odd one out?

    a) 3   b) 5   c) 9   d) 11

12 There are 250 pesetas to the pound. How many pesetas for £20?

    a) 5000   b) 500   c) 2500   d) 5500

13 Socks are £1.75 a pair or five pairs for £8. How much is the saving?

14 What is the average speed of a car that travels 120km in one and a half hours?

15 If an item costing £60 is reduced by 15% in a sale, what is the new price?

Set 3

? Test Yourself

The table show the grades in English and Maths at 16 + in 1979. The figures are percentages of total pupils in the year.

	Boys		Girls	
	Maths	English	Maths	English
Higher grades	28.9	30.1	22.1	39.1
Lower grades	40.1	44.3	45.4	41.8
Ungraded	7.8	4.7	9.8	3.0
Total entry	76.8	79.1	77.3	83.9

1 More girls got higher grades in Maths than boys. True/false?

2 More girls were graded in English than boys. True/false?

3 In which subject are boys most likely to be ungraded?

4 Are girls better at Maths or English?

5 Are you more likely to be ungraded in Maths or English?

Some number puzzles

6 I have a 4-litre, a 5-litre and a 7-litre jug. How can I measure 6 litres into the 7-litre jug?

7 From my bag of sweets I give ½ to Larry and ⅓ to John and I still have four sweets left. How many did I start with?

8 Express each of these as the sum of two consecutive numbers:

17   23   35   111

9 I want to boil an egg for 6 minutes, but I only have a 4-minute and a 5-minute egg timer. How can I do it?

Abstract ability

? Test Yourself

What comes next in each sequence?

1 I   =   III   ≡   ? |||||

2 ▬ ▭   ▐   ? ▯

3 ↑ ↖ ← ↙ ?

4 · ∴ ∴· ?

5 △ ■ ○ ▲ □ ?

6 ◉ ◱ ⊕ ▽ ◉ ?

7 **M M U M   M U M M   U M M M**   ?

8 Which is the odd one out?

a) ⊟ b) ◩ c) ◿ d) ▱ ?

9 ↿ is to ↾ as → is to?

10 ↾ is to ← as → is to?

11 ◳ is to ◩ as ◪ is to?

12 A B A is to **B A B** as **X T X** is to?

13 pat is to aa as dog is to?

14 ↑ is to ↓ ↓ to as → is to?

15 PEAT is to **TEAP** as **BOIT** is to?

Conclusions

We have covered a great deal of territory in a short time.
Here is a reminder of the key ideas and themes covered in
this book.

- We have looked at why the use of psychometric
  testing is increasingly used in a range of
  organisational contexts, from recruitment and
  selection through development to performance
  management and career counselling.
- We have shown how tests of aptitude and ability
  can give objective and detailed information about
  some of our important underlying cognitive skills.
- We have described the differences between tests of
  aptitude and ability and tests of personality and
  personal preferences.
- We have described that tests can examine a range
  of skills and capabilities, from learnt skills
  (attainment), through reasoning skills, to critical
  thinking skills.
- We have described the full range of aptitudes and
  abilities that can be tested, and have described in
  detail the three key areas of verbal, numerical and
  abstract ability.
- We have shown what is involved in each of these
  three key areas, and described how they are tested,
  including some of the more well known and well
  used tests.
- We have shown how the tests are scored and
  interpreted. In particular, scores for any individual

are compared to the scores for a comparable group of people (norms).

- You have had the opportunity to use the tests in this book to 'have a go', and to assist you in evaluating your own aptitudes and abilities.
- We have provided a section of practice material to help you to gain confidence and competence in these important areas.
- Finally, we have set out some ideas about how to go about developing your abilities in these areas.

If you want to look in even more depth at some of these topics you might be interested in the following forthcoming titles (due for publication in September 2000):

Test Your Numeracy Skills
Test Your Literacy Skills

Useful addresses

The British Psychological Society (BPS), 48 Princess Road East, LEICESTER LEI 7DR. Telephone 0116254 9568, Fax: 0116 2470787.

The Institute of Management (IM), Management House, Cottingham Road, Corby, Northants, NN17 1TT, Telephone 01536 204222.

The Institute of Personnel and Development (IPD), IPD House, Camp Road, LONDON SW19 4UX. Telephone 0181 971 9000.

Test suppliers and publishers

Assessment for Selection and Employment, Darville House, 2 Oxford Road East, Windsor, Berks SL4 1DF, Telephone 01753 850333.

Oxford Psychologists Press Ltd, Lambourne House, 311–321 Banbury Road, Oxford, 0X2 7JH, Telephone 01865 311353.

The Psychological Corporation, Foots Cray, High Street, Sidcup DA14 5HP.

Psytech International Ltd, The Grange, Church Road, Pulloxhill, Beds, MK45 5HE, Telephone 01525 720003.

Saville & Holdsworth Ltd, 3 AC Court, High Street, Thames Ditton, Surrey, KT7 0SR, Telephone 0181 398 4170.

The Test Agency, Cray House, Woodlands Road, Henley on Thames, Oxon, RG9 4AE, Telephone 01491 413413.

Further reading

BPS (1989) *Psychological Testing: Guidance for the User.* British Psychological Society, Leicester.

Cattell, R. B. (1978). *The Scientific Use of Factor Analysis in Behavioural and Life Sciences.* Plenum Press, New York.

Equal Opportunities Commission (1988) *Avoiding Sex Bias in Selection Testing: Guidance for Employers.* Manchester.

Gael, S. (1987) *The Job Analysis Handbook for Business, Industry and Government.* John Wiley and Sons.

IPD (1993) *The IPM Code on Psychological Testing.* IPD, Wimbledon.

Pearn, M. & Kandola, R. (1988) *Job Analysis – a Practical Guide for Managers.* IPM.

Smith, M. & Robertson, I. (1993) *Advances in Selection and Assessment.* John Wiley & Sons.

Answers

The test, page 50

Verbal ability

Set 1

1 c **2** b **3** d **4** a **5** d **6** BHMORSU **7** CASSADY
CASTLE CASTOR CATT CATTELL **8** POINTON
POROBIC PORTER POWELL POULSON **9** b **10** c
11 a **12** d **13** b **14** their **15** bear

Set 2

1 d **2** b **3** d **4** d **5** b **6** c **7** a **8** c **9** b **10** d

Set 3

1 b **2** b **3** c **4** b **5** c

Numerical ability

Set 1

1 41 **2** 26 **3** 27 **4** 64 **5** 4 **6** 13 **7** 28 **8** 26 **9** 84
10 135 **11** 104 **12** 98 **13** 7 **14** 21 **15** 5 **16** 15 **17** 5.5
18 13.4 **19** 15 **20** 2.5 **21** ¾ **22** ⁷⁄₁₀ or ⅕ **23** ⅘ or 1⅗
24 5 **25** 20p **26** 90p **27** £2.90 **28** £3.68 **29** 360
30 £5.51

Set 2

1 16 **2** 5 **3** 162 **4** 31 **5** 13 **6** c **7** a **8** c **9** d **10** a
11 e **12** 153 **13** d **14** a **15** b

Set 3

1 confidence tricks   **2** shoplifting   **3** false   **4** 7   **5** 4

Abstract ability

1 O   **2** O   **3** ←   **4** | **5** XIX   **6** ⌐   **7** TOTOO   **8** d   **9** c
10 ←   **11** ◿   **12** FF   **13** ⌐   **14** XTTX   **15** IHG

Practice

Verbal ability

Set 1

1 b **2** a **3** c **4** a **5** a **6** AEIKMST **7** MORANT
MORGAN   MORONEY   MORRIS   MOULTON
8   POWROZNYK   POZYLO   PRAJAPATI
PRAXMARER   PREMJI **9** c **10** d **11** b **12** d **13** b
14 has **15** hail

Set 2

1 d **2** b **3** a **4** b **5** c **6** red **7** pro **8** a **9** c **10** d

Set 3

1 a **2** b **3** c **4** a **5** b

Numerical ability

Set 1

1 27 **2** 30 **3** 41 **4** 61 **5** 7 **6** 16 **7** 16 **8** 45 **9** 65
10 126 **11** 135 **12** 141 **13** 11 **14** 13 **15** 4 **16** 23 **17** 5.5
18 10.4 **19** 12 **20** 8 **21** $\frac{7}{6}$ or $1\frac{1}{6}$ **22** $\frac{1}{20}$ **23** $\frac{6}{5}$ or $1\frac{1}{5}$
24 22 **25** 50p **26** £1.10 **27** £5.50 **28** £6 **29**   300 tonnes
30 £36.50

Set 2

1 13 **2** 32 **3** 203 **4** 7.5 **5** 162 **6** c **7** d **8** a **9** b
10 d **11** d **12** a **13** 75p **14** 80 kmph **15** £51

Set 3

1 false **2** true **3** Maths **4**   English **5** Maths

Number puzzles

6 Fill the 5-litre jug and empy it into the 4-litre jug. This
leaves 1 litre in the 5-litre jug. Pour it into the 7-litre jug.
Refill the 5-litre jug and pour it into the 7-litre jug,
making 6 litres in all.

7 12

8 8+7   11+12   17+18   55+56

9 Set both timers off. When the 4-minute timer stops, start
boiling the egg. When the 5-minute timer stops (after 1
minute), restart it and boil the egg until it finishes.

Abstract ability

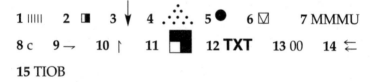

1 ||||| **2** ◨   **3** ↓   **4** .·.·.   **5** ●   **6** ▱   **7** MMMU

8 c   **9** →   **10** ⌐   **11** ◤   **12 TXT**   **13** 00   **14** ⇐

15 TIOB

Further *Test Your ...* titles from Hodder & Stoughton and the Institute of Management, all at £6.99

0 340 78006 1	Test Your Personality	❑
0 340 78050 9	Test Your Management Style	❑
0 340 78169 9	Test Your Management Skills	❑
0 340 78208 0	Test Your Leadership Skills	❑

Publishing in September 2000:

0 340 78287 0	Test Your Financial Awareness	❑
0 340 78288 9	Test Your Literacy	❑
0 340 78289 7	Test Your Numeracy	❑
0 340 78290 0	Test Your Potential	❑

All Hodder & Stoughton books are available from your local bookshop or can be ordered direct from the publisher. Just tick the titles you want and fill in the form below. Prices and availability subject to change without notice.

To: Hodder & Stoughton Ltd, Cash Sales Department, Bookpoint, 78 Milton Park, Abingdon, Oxon OX14 4TD. If you have a credit card you may order by
telephone – 01235 400414
        fax – 01235 400454
E-mail address: orders@bookpoint.co.uk

Please enclose a cheque or postal order made payable to Bookpoint Ltd to the value of the cover price and allow the following for postage and packaging:

UK & BFPO: £4.30 for one book; £6.30 for two books; £8.30 for three books.

OVERSEAS & EIRE: £4.80 for one book; £7.10 for 2 or 3 books (surface mail).

Name: ....

Address: ....

....

....

If you would prefer to pay by credit card, please complete:

Please debit my Visa/Mastercard/Diner's Card/American Express (delete as appropriate) card no:

❑ ❑ ❑ ❑ ❑ ❑ ❑ ❑ ❑ ❑ ❑ ❑ ❑ ❑ ❑ ❑ ❑ ❑

Signature .... Expiry date ....

Further *Successful Business in a Week* **titles from Hodder & Stoughton and the Institute of Management all at £6.99**

0 340 71205 8	Appraisals in a Week	❏	0 340 65503 8	Managing Change in a Week ❏
0 340 70546 9	Assertiveness in a Week	❏	0 340 74757 9	Marketing in a Week ❏
0 340 71197 3	Benchmarking in a Week	❏	0 340 47579 7	Marketing Plans in a Week ❏
0 340 57640 5	Budgeting in a Week	❏	0 340 57466 6	Market Research in a Week ❏
0 340 74751 X	Bullying at Work in a Week	❏	0 340 60894 3	Meetings in a Week ❏
0 340 72077 8	Business Growth in a Week	❏	0 340 74241 0	Memory Techniques in a Week ❏
0 340 70540 X	Business on the Internet in a Week	❏	0 340 61137 5	Mentoring in a Week ❏
0 340 71199 X	Business Plans in a Week	❏	0 340 71174 4	Mind Maps® in a Week ❏
0 340 59813 1	Business Writing in a Week	❏	0 340 73761 1	Motivation in a Week ❏
0 340 71200 7	Communication at Work in a Week	❏	0 340 70545 0	Negotiating in a Week ❏
0 340 62032 3	Computing for Business in a Week	❏	0 340 64341 2	Networking in a Week ❏
0 340 73781 6	Consultancy in a Week	❏	0 340 71123 X	Neuro-Linguistic Programming
0 340 74752 8	Credit Control in a Week	❏		in a Week ❏
0 340 71196 5	Customer Care in a Week	❏	0 340 73812 X	Office Feng Shui in a Week ❏
0 340 70543 4	CVs in a Week	❏	0 340 72073 5	Personal Investment in a Week ❏
0 340 72076 X	Dealing with Difficult People		0 340 70541 8	Planning Your Own Career
	in a Week	❏		in a Week ❏
0 340 63154 6	Decision Making in a Week	❏	0 340 70544 2	Presentation in a Week ❏
0 340 73762 X	Delegation in a Week	❏	0 340 71208 2	Process Management in a Week ❏
0 340 62741 7	Direct Mail in a Week	❏	0 340 70539 6	Project Management in a Week ❏
0 340 75336 6	E-commerce in a Week	❏	0 340 64761 2	Problem Solving in a Week ❏
0 340 73048 X	E-mail in a Week	❏	0 340 73780 8	Psychometric Testing in a Week ❏
0 340 64330 7	Empowerment in a Week	❏	0 340 56479 2	Public Relations in a Week ❏
0 340 66374 X	Environmental Management		0 340 71206 6	Purchasing in a Week ❏
	in a Week	❏	0 340 73816 2	Recruitment in a Week ❏
0 340 71192 2	Finance for Non-Financial		0 340 71198 1	Report Writing in a Week ❏
	Managers in a Week	❏	0 340 70538 8	Selling in a Week ❏
0 340 71189 2	Flexible Working in a Week	❏	0 340 67397 4	Selling on the Internet in a Week ❏
0 340 67925 5	Fundraising and Sponsorship		0 340 65504 6	Statistics in a Week ❏
	in a Week	❏	0 340 72494 3	Strategy in a Week ❏
0 340 71204 X	Going Freelance in a Week	❏	0 340 71201 5	Stress Management in a Week ❏
0 340 65487 2	Human Resource Management		0 340 70542 6	Succeeding at Interviews in a Week ❏
	in a Week	❏	0 340 71207 4	Teambuilding in a Week ❏
0 340 74287 9	Information Overload in a Week	❏	0 340 70547 7	Time Management in a Week ❏
0 340 74756 0	Interviewing in a Week	❏	0 340 71191 4	Total Quality Management
0 340 71179 5	Intranets in a Week	❏		in a Week ❏
0 340 63152 X	Introducing Management in a Week	❏	0 340 75785 X	Tough Interview Questions in a
0 340 71203 i	Introduction to Bookkeeping			Week ❏
	and Accounting in a Week	❏	0 340 71195 7	Training in a Week ❏
0340 753374	Investors in People in a Week	❏	0 340 62102 8	VAT in a Week ❏
0 340 71202 3	Leadership in a Week	❏	0 340 67905 0	Virtual Organisation in a Week ❏
0 340 71173 6	Management Gurus in a Week	❏	0 340 70508 6	Web Sites in a Week ❏

All Hodder & Stoughton books are available from your local bookshop or can be ordered direct from the publisher. Just tick the titles you want and fill in the form below. Prices and availability subject to change without notice.

To: Hodder & Stoughton Ltd, Cash Sales Department, Bookpoint, 39 Milton Park, Abingdon, Oxon, OX14 4TD. If you have a credit card you may order by telephone – 01235 400414.

E-mail address: orders@bookpoint.co.uk

Please enclose a cheque or postal order made payable to Bookpoint Ltd to the value of the cover price and allow the following for postage and packaging:

UK & BFPO: £4.30 for one book; £6.30 for two books; £8.30 for three books.

OVERSEAS & EIRE: £4.80 for one book; £7.10 for 2 or 3 books (surface mail).

Name: ....

Address: ....

....

If you would prefer to pay by credit card, please complete:

Please debit my Visa/Mastercard/Diner's Card/American Express (delete as appropriate) card no:

☐ ☐ ☐ ☐ ☐ ☐ ☐ ☐ ☐ ☐ ☐ ☐ ☐ ☐ ☐ ☐

Signature .... Expiry Date ....